Respect
the Queen

By

Michelle Rogers

Copyright © 2021 Michelle Rogers

All rights reserved. No part of this publication may be reproduced, distributed, or transmitted in any form or by any means, including photocopying, recording, or other electronic or mechanical methods, without the prior written permission of the publisher, except in the case of brief quotations embodied in critical reviews and certain other noncommercial uses permitted by copyright law.

ISBN-13: 978-1-951300-23-4

Liberation's Publishing ~ West Point, Mississippi

Dedication

to those who love love

Table of Content

Respect the Queen 7

Thoughts Are Deep 11

Myself 15

Nothing But Love 19

Blind Love 23

I Feel In Love With You 27

Love at First Sight 31

The Love In My Heart 35

In This Thing Called Life 39

Words Without Action 43

One Day 47

Respect the Queen

Never building me up yet so easy to knock me down.

You the one that say you love me but I feel enemy vibes when you around

Having your back, I always have for you but when it comes to defending me that's impossible for you to do.

It's mind vs true colors

Reality vs heart and honesty

Just the thought tares me completely apart!!!

My love may run deep and my love for you may be strong

Most importantly I'm a beautiful black queen that don't deserve to be treated wrong

Journal Entry

Date:

Thoughts Are Deep

I place my thoughts on paper cause when I speak I'm never heard.

In this life I've felt mistreated

And somewhat silently beaten

I keep in an awful lot and

At times with this life I've even wanted it to stop...

I been let down plenty times and yet feeling used and when it comes to my heart it's been very well abused...

My heart hold scars and my soul hold pain my head hold thoughts and with pen and paper I explain

Never take a loving heart and treat it like trash cause somewhere down the line you yourself is bound to crash !!!!

Journal Entry

_____

_____

_____

_____

_____

Date:

Myself

Believe in me for I am uniquely made

With an ingenious mind and A

Personality that's rare, when it comes to meeting strangers I don't even compare

A heart that's pure as gold

Even though I'm living in a world so cold

A smile that gives you peace

In the mist of your storm

A touch that warms your heart and yet mend your soul

make you stronger by the minute and impossible for you to fold.

Believe in me for I'll tell you no wrong cause GOD is the one who keeps me strong

The Spirit of love and the different glows that people see let's me know that GOD is yet at work and working through me

Journal Entry

_____
_____
_____
_____
_____
_____
_____
_____
_____
_____
_____
_____
_____

Date:

Nothing But Love

Questioning my loyalty no need for you to do.

Cause I loved you from the start and stayed true to you.

Time passed and I felt as if you let me down

But two seconds of your voice always removed the frown

I'll always love you near I'll yet love you far

Understand that I love you simply for who you are

Loving you through the good and during the bad

I loved you even harder on the days you made me sad

I never loved for what you have nor for what you do

I loved you on the strength and vibe I felt from you.

Journal Entry

_____
_____
_____
_____
_____
_____
_____
_____
_____
_____
_____
_____
_____
_____

Date:

Blind Love

Loving someone who don't truly love you back

Is like pulling groceries from an empty sack

Getting back with someone who don't appreciate you from the start

Is opening up hurt for your very own heart

Letting go of what you love can definitely hurt you to your soul

And sometimes letting go can make you better as a whole

Know who you are and never settle for less,

When GOD made you he made the very best!

Journal Entry

Date:

I Feel In Love With You

My eyes were on you as far back as I can remember.

Every time I saw you… my heart oh so tender

It seemed like you vanished for a little while… but you were only a few miles away.

My eyes on you

I couldn't resist any longer, but with a simple, "Hey!"

I became much stronger

A signal from my eye

I think you could tell

my my my

You had me hypnotized under a spell.

Being able to see you night after night began to make my days oh so bright

The way you treated me and things you did, I couldn't help but fall in love with you again.

Journal Entry

_____
_____
_____
_____
_____
_____
_____
_____
_____
_____
_____
_____
_____

Date:

Love at First Sight

Love at first sight I strongly disagree

Love at first sight in my opinion it's lust to me

Love can be strong and lust can too

Be careful not to let it confuse you

Love is a feeling that's hard to explain and in my opinion love is actions that's very much untamed

Lust has no patience

Lust can feel so real

Lust only see you for what you can do and lust will also say I love you

Some people come in your life as a great blessing and some people come in your life to teach you a life lesson

Love is a Lifetime Love Overcome Love always value and Love is everlasting..

Journal Entry

___
___
___
___
___
___
___
___
___
___
___
___
___
___
___
___

Date:

The Love In My Heart

The love in my heart just for you

The love in my heart yes it's true

Never from my heart will this love go away

Always, this love in my heart is here to stay.

Journal Entry

Date:

In This Thing Called Life

In this thing called life we have decisions to make.

Sometimes they are made on time and sometimes they are made too late. Sometimes the decision you make can very well be a mistake.

In this thing called life we have plenty of options.

An option to live with hate or an option to be positive and live life great. An option to be weak or an option to be strong.

but living life with GOD it's impossible to go wrong.

Sometimes in life we get talked about bad.

In this thing called life people will work

to bring your warm heart and smiling face to a level of sad.

In this thing called life you never know what you will face.

Acknowledge GOD, stay strong, and always keep the faith.

Journal Entry

_____
_____
_____
_____
_____
_____
_____
_____
_____
_____
_____
_____

Date:

Words Without Action

You said that you loved me, but didn't show any actions.

So when your feelings got hurt I didn't show any compassion.

Around people…

You treated me like dirt

And didn't even care about my feelings being hurt.

You said that you loved me but constantly caused my heart pain.

Most days was less sunshine and more storm and rain.

I loved you like no other but loving me is where you lacked.

So by all means I had to fall back.

Journal Entry

Date:

One Day

Just really getting to know you but I'm feeling your vibe.

Trying to let this friendship go a little further to see what your heart is like inside.

One day I wish to feel your arms hold me tight.

With love, care and compassion as for my body do it right.

Explaining you with words I can never be through.

I wish one day wish there would be something special with me and You

Journal Entry

_____
_____
_____
_____
_____

Date:

www.ingramcontent.com/pod-product-compliance
Lightning Source LLC
Chambersburg PA
CBHW062031120526
44592CB00037B/2198